The Origin Of The Alphabet

Elissa Uncovers...

Written by
Nancy Zakhour

Illustrated by
Oana R. Gheorghe

D1128837

ISBN: 979-8-9863016-0-0 (Paperback)
ISBN: 979-8-9863016-1-7 (Hardback)

Illustrated by Oana Gheorghe

To our parents and grandparents,
for giving us all the love and hope in the world.

To our children,
the children of the world,
you are our future.

One day, Grandmother asked Elissa to go into the attic and bring down a bright brown trunk.

Elissa did so.

Grandmother opened the trunk and showed Elissa an immense pile of letters and cards.

Some of them were from Elissa
when she was much younger,
but there were others—so many others.

They had been sent to Grandmother by her
parents, her brothers and sisters, her children,
nieces and nephews, and friends.
They had been sent from all over the world.

They had been sent from all over the world.

Grandmother and her family had traveled almost everywhere.

"Whoa!" exclaimed Elissa.

"There's a whole history in here," said Grandmother.

"And when you're grown up and traveling all over the world, I can put all the letters from you in here too."

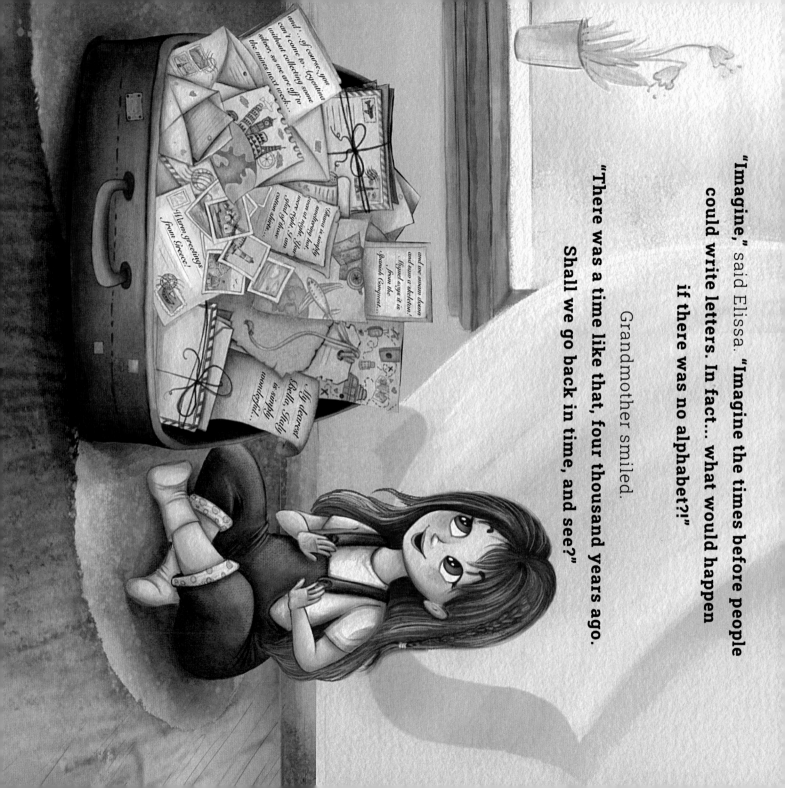

"Imagine," said Elissa. "Imagine the times before people could write letters. In fact... what would happen if there was no alphabet?!"

Grandmother smiled.

"There was a time like that, four thousand years ago. Shall we go back in time, and see?"

"Yes, please, Grandmother!"

Elissa might be a big girl now,
but she still loved her grandmother's stories.

"Once upon a time," began Grandmother...

*...Elissa was a sea merchant,
sailing across the known world,
which was a lot smaller than it is now.*

Elissa's people were Phoenicians and they were merchants
who loved adventure, finding new things,
and making trades with people in every country.

Phoenicia was a tiny strip of land, cuddled along the curve
where the Near East met the Mediterranean Sea.

With unforgiving desert behind them, they looked to the sea and built special ships for sailing, learned how to navigate by the stars, and how to trade.

It didn't matter whether they were selling the finest wines to Egypt, expensive dyes from Mogador in Morocco to textile manufacturers, or the homegrown, majestic, and sweetly scented cedar logs that were their best products.

Elissa smiled when the Greek coast came into view. **"Excellent,"** she said. **"We've made good time."**

As the ship cruised regally into port, Elissa waved when she saw her friend, Petros.

He was always ready to buy her rich and royal purple fabric that was the envy of the Mediterranean.

"I'm so happy to see you, my **Phoenician friend**" said Petros as he came panting up the gangway.

(The ancient Greeks sometimes called the Canaanites "Phoenicians.")

The Phoenicians were the only people to have found a source for the dark Tyrian purple dye, and their clothing and bolts of fabric always sold for an excellent price.

"I'm desperate for more of your silver items. My wife's father has sent word that he's coming to visit, and I need to impress him."

"Oh!" Elissa clapped her hands to her mouth. "I didn't bring a lot this time. I brought extra fabric instead."

"Oh, well, that's a shame. I'll take all the silver you have," said Petros. "And I'll look at your textiles too."

It was the first time Elissa had sold out of silver before the ship was fully tied up.

She was pleased to make a good profit on the silver, but sad that her friend had not been able to get what he wanted from her. It was annoying, she thought, that there was no way Petros could have sent a message to her in between voyages, telling her what he needed.

A messenger wouldn't be able to do it, not with many miles of sea in the way. If only there were a method of communication...

"*I wonder,*" mused Elissa. There were only so many sounds in words after all... She wondered if she could devise a system of drawn symbols in which each one represented a sound as she watched a herd of cattle ambling past, mooing and swishing their tails.

"Aleph,"

mused Elissa.

(Aleph means cow or oxen)

"That's an 'ah' sound. Any time I say a word where there's an 'ah' sound, I'll draw a cow's head."

She sketched a simple cow's head
in the dirt in front of her.

Just then, an irate mother chased her son up the road. He was two years old, laughing wildly, and running as fast as he could.

He was also naked and covered with soapy bubbles: he had escaped from his bath!

"Get into the house now!" shouted his mother.

"The whole town is looking at you!"

They were—but they were laughing, and the little boy continued to run away from his mother, shedding soapy bubbles as he went.

"**Bet**,"
said Elissa.
(Bet means house)

Bet
B

"So, if I think of a house, like this... and call this sound 'buh,' then little house shapes will always mean 'buh'. There. That's two sounds done."

Elissa carried on like this until she had a symbol
for every sound she could think of.

This is what her list looked like.

Then, carefully, before someone could walk over it,
or the rain could wash it away, she drew her brand new
"alphabet" on a piece of animal skin.

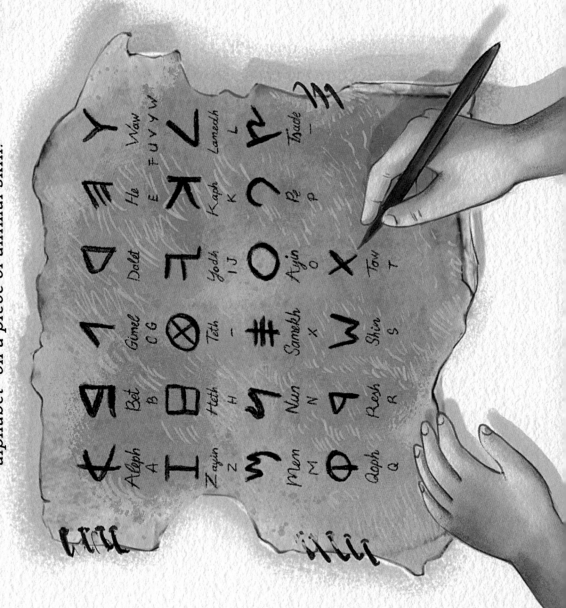

That night, she went to supper with Petros and his wife. She brought a clay tablet on which she had written her alphabet. She explained it to them while they ate, and they were very excited.

"So next time I need extra supplies, I can send one of these tablets to you, saying what I need, and you will know what to bring with you?"

"Yes, exactly," said Elissa.

Elissa traveled far and wide throughout the world—if you could get there by sea, the Phoenicians visited.

Everywhere she went, she took copies of her tablets with her alphabet pressed into them.

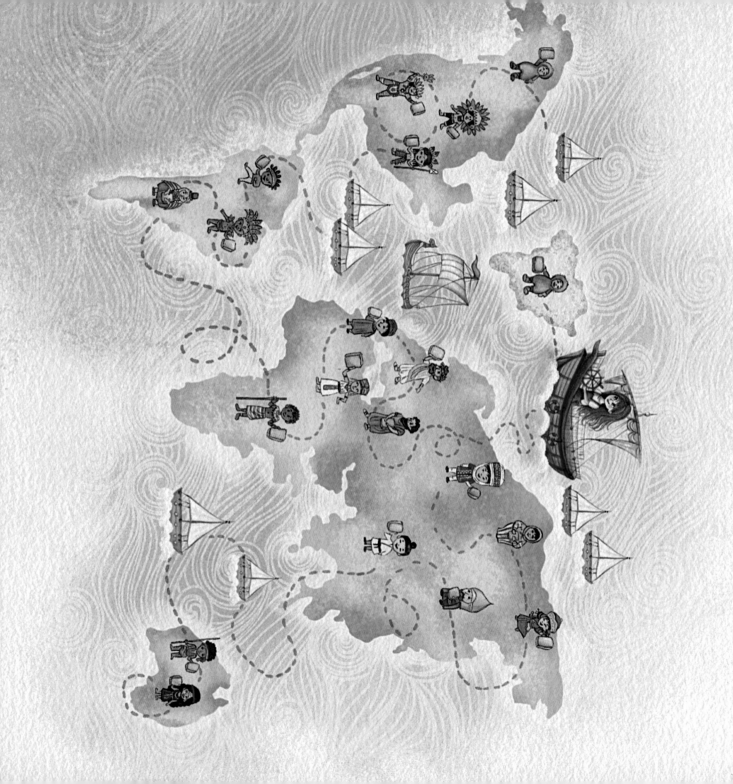

People were very happy to have a sensible way of recording things that happened, and eventually there were many variations of alphabets. Soon, Petros had two to deal with: Elissa's Phoenician and a brand-new Greek alphabet.

Now, he was able to order a lot of cedar in good time to impress his grumpy father-in-law, so he was very happy; even though reading and writing were new skills that he had to learn and teach to others...

..."And before long, many different nations had their own version of an alphabet, and there were new industries like paper making and the invention of pens and pencils," said Grandmother.

"And all of those has led to this."

"That's amazing!" exclaimed Elissa.
"Now I can write stories and letters, read all about
people everywhere, and learn about our ancestors
who lived thousands of years ago—alphabets
are the most amazing invention ever!"

And so they are. Don't you agree?

About The Author
Nancy Zakhour

Nancy Zakhour has a background in engineering and currently works in the finance and energy industry. Nancy grew up in Lebanon before moving to the US, and her experiences have made her passionate about telling stories that connect people from different cultural backgrounds. As a child, she was told stories by her parents and grandparents that filled her imagination, and ever since, they have held a special place in her heart. Her family recounted their own experiences as well as told her traditional stories that had been passed down verbally through the generations. Nancy wanted to share these stories with the world.

Traveling the world led Nancy to understand that her culture and tradition had its own unique perspective and tales to tell, and that these were often unknown to others. She became determined to reveal the unseen treasures of her Lebanese-Armenian heritage. Touching people's hearts and minds is centrally important to Nancy. Telling the stories of her father—who was a gifted storyteller—is what inspired Nancy to become a children's author. Making an impact on readers, especially children, is the best way she can pay tribute to her beloved parents and grandparents. Nancy is multilingual, fluent in Arabic, English, French, and Armenian. Her background and experiences have gifted her the strong desire to learn more about different cultures and to raise awareness of them by telling their untold stories.

Made in the USA
Coppell, TX
27 November 2022

87228097R00029